Billy and Tom went to play in the pond.

Milly and Tilly went to play on the log.

Tilly fell off the log.

Tilly fell in the mud.

Milly went to help Tilly.

Milly fell in the mud.

Billy went to help Tilly and Milly.

Billy fell in the mud.

Tom went to the hut to get mum and dad.

Mum and dad went to help the little pigs ...

... but ... mum and dad fell in the mud.